MW01089818

THE RUBY WOMAN

A BIBLE STUDY OF PROVERBS 31:10-31

JUANITA HALL

Cover Art by Dave Chiarelli

ISBN: 1535187638
ISBN-13: 9781535187633

DEDICATION

To all the Ruby Women at Calvary Rio Rancho. You have each been used by our Lord to help shape my understanding of this portion of God's Word, and to beautifully influence my own spiritual journey.

Juanita Hall

CONTENTS

ACKNOWLEDGMENTS

Thanks especially to Megan Weeks, whose own desire to study this topic prompted me to get busy and put my thoughts down on paper. Many thanks also to K.G. Powderly for fine job editing and formatting, despite the distinctly female quality of the subject.

All citations of Scripture from the…
- New King James Version (NKJV) © 1982 by Thomas Nelson, Inc.
- New International Version (NIV) © 1973 by New York Bible Society International
- New American Standard Bible (NASB) © 1960, 1962, 1963, 1968, 1971, 1972, 1973, 1975 and 1977 by The Lockman Foundation, La Habra, Ca.
- New Living Translation (NLT) © copyright © 1996, 2004, 2015 by Tyndale House Foundation
- Amplified Translation (AMP) © Copyright © 1965, 1987, & 2015 by The Lockman Foundation.
- The Message © Copyright © 1993, 1994, 1995, 1996, 2000, 2001,& 2002 by NavPress Publishing Group.

Other citations from…
- *Be Skillful*, by Warren W. Wiersbe ©1995 by Victor Books/SP Publications, Inc. Wheaton, IL 60187.
- *Commentary on Proverbs*, by George Lawson ©1980 by Kregel Publications, Grand Rapids, MI 49501.
- *The Communicator's Commentary on Proverbs*, by David A. Hubbard, ©1989 by Word, Inc., Dallas, TX 75234.
- *Exploring Proverbs Volume Two*, by John Phillips, ©2002 by Kregel Publications, Grand Rapids, MI 49501.
- *Practical Proverbs for Your Problems*, by David Hocking, ©1991 by Promise Publishing, Orange, CA 92667.
- *Proverbs*, by Kenneth T. Aitken, ©1986 by Westminster Press, Philadelphia, PA.
- *Proverbs*, by H. A. Ironside, ©1989 by Loizeaux Brothers, Neptune, NJ 07753.
- *Proverbs*, by Charles Bridges, ©1987 by Banner of Truth Trust, Carlisle, PA 17013.
- *Proverbs*, by Derek Kidner, ©1964 by The Tyndale Press, Downers Grove, IL 60515.
- *Selected Studies From Proverbs*, by Charles R. Swindoll, ©1999, 1994 by Insight for Living, Anaheim, CA 92806.
- *Studies in Proverbs*, by William Arnot, ©1978 by Kregel Publications, Grand Rapids, MI 49501.
- *The Wisdom of Proverbs*, by Bob Beasley, ©1999 by Legacy Press, Blackwood, NJ 08012.

1

MEET THE RUBY WOMAN

Who can find a virtuous wife? For her worth is far above rubies.

Proverbs 31:10 (NKJV)

Besides "The Ruby Woman," what other titles would be appropriate for this section of Scripture?

_____

_____

_____

Verses 10-31 of Proverbs are written as an *acrostic*. What is an acrostic, and what would be the purpose for writing it that way?

_____

_____

_____

_____

Whose words are being quoted in this poem?

_____

Have you instructed your children in the qualities to look for in a mate? If so, how do they match up with Lemuel's mom's instruction?

_____

_____

_____

_____

What do you think most young people today usually look for in a boyfriend or girlfriend?

_____

_____

_____

_____

How do the following verses speak to your heart?
Proverbs 1:8

_____

_____

_____

_____

Proverbs 6:20

_____

_____

_____

_____

Proverbs 4:3

_____

_____

_____

_____

_____

Do you think of your mother as wise and good? _____

How do your children (including those who look up to you as a "spiritual mother") describe you to others?

_____

_____

_____

Do you think that your son hopes to find a woman "just like Mom" to marry?

_____

_____

_____

Of whom do the following passages speak?
2 Timothy 1:5

_____

_____

_____

2 Timothy 3:15

_____

_____

_____

In reading through Proverbs 31:10-31, do you believe this tribute is to a woman who displayed these characteristics every single day, and did what is described? Why or why not?

_____

_____

_____

In future lessons we will study this amazing woman's worth, works, wisdom, witnesses, and worship. What questions do you already have?

_____

_____

_____

_____

2

HER WORTH

Who can find a virtuous wife? For her worth is far above rubies.
Proverbs 31:10 (NKJV)

After you answer all the questions below, come back and write a banner heading for Proverbs 31:10.

_____

_____

_____

What conclusions do you draw from the question asked in this verse?

_____

_____

_____

_____

If you died and your loved ones had to hire people to take your place, who would they have to hire, and how much would it cost them?

_____

_____

_____

What is the going rate for a perfect ruby today?

_____

How much value does our society place on homemakers with home businesses today?

_____

_____

_____

_____

What insight do you gain about the value of women from Proverbs 18:22?

_____

_____

_____

_____

What else does Proverbs 8:35 compare in value with finding a good wife, and infer is a sign of God's blessings?

_____

_____

_____

What would your husband trade for his right arm? Have you helped him to think of you as that valuable? Does Ephesians 5:28 shed light on this?

_____

_____

_____

Which of the following verses stands out to you and why?

Proverbs 19:14

_____

_____

_____

Ecclesiastes 9:9

_____

_____

_____

_____

_____

How many wives and concubines did Solomon have, according to 1 Kings 11:3? What does King Solomon express in Ecclesiastes 7:27-28? How are these two things related?

_____

_____

_____

_____

_____

_____

_____

What else does the Bible say is more precious than rubies? Look up the Hebrew word translated *rubies* in the KJV and do a word search to discover the answer.

_____

_____

_____

_____

_____

Do a word search on the word translated *virtuous* in the King James (KJV). Where else is this same word used in the Bible?

What insights do you gain from looking at the following verses?
Proverbs 12:4

_____

_____

_____

_____

_____

Proverbs 31:29

_____

_____

_____

_____

_____

_____

Ecclesiastes 12:3

_____

_____

_____

_____

_____

Genesis 47:5-6

_____

_____

_____

_____

_____

Exodus 18:21

_____

_____

_____

_____

_____

Deuteronomy 3:18-19

_____

_____

_____

_____

_____

Deuteronomy 8:18

_____

_____

_____

_____

_____

Joshua 10:7

_____

_____

_____

_____

_____

Judges 6:12

_____

_____

_____

_____

_____

Judges 11:1

_____

_____

_____

_____

_____

_____

Ruth 2:1

_____

_____

_____

_____

_____

_____

1 Samuel 9:1

_____

_____

_____

_____

_____

1 Samuel 16:18

_____

_____

_____

_____

_____

_____

1 Samuel 31:11-12

_____

_____

_____

_____

_____

2 Samuel 17:10

_____

_____

_____

_____

_____

2 Samuel 22:33

_____

_____

_____

_____

_____

_____

1 Kings 11:28

_____

_____

_____

_____

_____

2 Kings 5:1

_____

_____

_____

_____

1 Chronicles 12:8

_____

_____

_____

_____

_____

2 Chronicles 26:17

_____

_____

_____

_____

_____

_____

2 Chronicles 32:21

_____

_____

_____

_____

What meaning do we usually give to the word _virtuous_?

_____

_____

_____

Since 1 Peter calls the woman "the weaker partner" (1 Peter 3:7); weaker in _what sense_?

_____

_____

_____

_____

What was it in Ruth that made Boaz describe her as a virtuous woman?

_____

_____

_____

Do you think your husband thinks of you as a blessing and treasure, and as a valiant woman of strength from God?

_____

What changes in your actions and attitudes are you asking God to transform in you?

_____

_____

_____

What steps are you willing to implement into your life in order to become a woman of virtue?

_____

_____

_____

_____

Which other women in the Bible do you think of as having this courageous strength of character?

_____ _____ _____

_____ _____ _____

_____ _____ _____

Which would you rather have: wealth (nice home, nicely decorated and landscaped; nice car; the ability to get your nails painted and your hair done every few weeks; the ability to pay for a good college education for yourself and private school for your children; pretty jewelry; nice clothes, etc.) or richness of godly character? Privately, get honest with God, and ask Him to give you a passion for godly character. As the Lord leads, share with the women in your group what you believe God is showing you.

Juanita Hall

3

HER FRIENDSHIP

The heart of her husband safely trusts her; So he will have no lack of gain.
Proverbs 31:11 (NKJV)

After you answer all the questions below, come back and give a banner heading for Proverbs 31:11.

When your husband is not around, do you think he worries about what you say, what you are doing or not doing, and how you are spending your time or the household money?

Are you concerned that your husband be able to trust in you completely?

Do you do as you think he would like you to do when he's not there?

Read the story about Achan in Joshua, Chapter 7. Wouldn't it be awful to find out in heaven that Achan's wife was covetous and selfishly indulgent—a woman who encouraged him in his greedy sin? What were the consequences of his disobedience?

Read Acts 5:1-11. Do you think Ananias had confidence in his wife Sapphira? Was that a good thing? Why or why not?

_____

_____

_____

What does Ephesians 5:15-16 tell you about the good management of your time?

_____

_____

_____

We've already emphasized the value of obtaining a good wife. Proverbs 19:14, describes her by the specific word *prudent*. What does *prudent* mean? Does it describe YOU?

_____

_____

_____

In Titus 2:4 women are instructed to have the friendship kind of love (Greek— *philandros*) for their husbands. Do you think your husband thinks of you as one of his best friends? Look up the following verses and write down some of the qualities of a loving friendship.

Proverbs 17:17

_____

_____

_____

Proverbs 18:24

_____

_____

_____

_____

Proverbs 19:22

_____

_____

_____

Proverbs 20:6

_____

_____

_____

In giving instructions to Timothy concerning qualifications for church leaders, what does Paul say about their wives? Does that describe you?
1 Timothy 3:11

_____

_____

_____

Juanita Hall

4

HER ATTITUDE

She does him good and not evil All the days of her life.

Proverbs 31:12 (NKJV)

After you answer all the questions below, come back and give a banner heading to Proverbs 31:12.

_____

_____

When you were first married, how did you treat your husband? Did you "do him good"? How long does verse twelve say wives should be doing that?

_____

_____

_____

_____

All of the following verses use the same words for "good" and "evil" (or their NT equivalents) that are in Proverbs 31:12. Which of these verses stands out to you and why?

Deuteronomy 30:15-16

_____

_____

_____

_____

_____

_____

Psalm 37:27

Psalm 34:11-16

1 Peter 3:10-12

Proverbs 11:27

_____

_____

_____

_____

_____

Proverbs 14:19

_____

_____

_____

_____

Proverbs 14:22

_____

_____

_____

_____

_____

Proverbs 15:15

_____

_____

_____

_____

_____

_____

Ecclesiastes 12:14

_____

_____

_____

_____

_____

2 Corinthians 5:10

_____

_____

_____

_____

_____

_____

Amos 5:14-15

_____

_____

_____

_____

_____

_____

Romans 12:21

_____

_____

_____

_____

_____

Romans 16:19

_____

_____

_____

_____

_____

_____

1 Thessalonians 5:15

_____

_____

_____

_____

_____

_____

3 John 1:11

_____

_____

_____

_____

_____

When Job sought to show patience in the face of his suffering, did his wife do him good or evil? What was Job's response to her? Read about it in Job 2:7-10.

_____

_____

_____

_____

_____

Genesis 2:18 in the King James and American Standard Versions say that God made a *help meet* for Adam. What does *help meet* mean?

_____

_____

_____

_____

_____

Do you struggle with the idea of being your husband's helper? Look up the Hebrew word for *help meet* and see where else in the Bible this same word is used. Share one or two verses that stand out to you.

_____

_____

_____

_____

What would be the opposite of *helper*?

_____

Write or type out the following verses. Is the woman in each described as a "helper"? If not, how is she described?

Proverbs 19:13b

_____

_____

_____

Proverbs 21:9, & 19

_____

_____

_____

_____

Proverbs 25:24

_____

_____

_____

Proverbs 27:15

_____

_____

_____

In Proverbs 14:1, the word *house* can also mean *family* (CEV & NCV) as in *the house of David*. List at least 10 ways that the wise woman helps her family to flourish and then at least 10 ways the foolish woman causes deterioration. Are you constructing or demolishing?

_____

_____

_____

_____

_____

5

HER DILIGENCE

She seeks wool and flax, And willingly works with her hands.

Proverbs 31:13 (NKJV)

After you answer all the questions below, come back and give a banner heading to verse 13.

_____

_____

What is wool and flax for, and why would the woman in verse 13 seek it?

_____

_____

What are the two verbs in verse 13? Describe how *you* do both in supplying clothing for your family.

Verb #1:

_____

_____

_____

Verb #2:

_____

_____

_____

_____

What descriptive word(s) express *how* the godly woman works, with what kind of attitude? What would be the opposite? Which describes you?

_____

_____

_____

_____

_____

_____

_____

Look up the following verses. Choose the one that stands out to you most, and write why.
Psalm 40:8 ■ Proverbs 10:4 ■ Proverbs 21:25 ■ Ecclesiastes 9:10 ■ 2 Corinthians 9:7 ■ Ephesians 6:7 ■ Colossians 3:23 ■ Ephesians 4:28 ■ 1 Thessalonians 4:11-12 ■ 2 Thessalonians 3:10

_____

_____

_____

_____

Do you enjoy weaving or knitting and sewing? If not, does that mean that you are not a godly woman?

_____

6

HER SKILL

She is like the merchant ships, She brings her food from afar.

Proverbs 31:14 (NKJV)

After you answer all the questions below, come back and give a banner heading to verse 14.

_____

_____

Eugene Peterson's paraphrase, *The Message* says, **"She's like a trading ship that sails to faraway places and brings back exotic surprises."** Do you ever provide "exotic surprises" for your family or do you just do the minimum in food preparation, fixing the same safe meals over and over again? Share an "exotic surprise" recipe with the group.

_____

_____

_____

Do you ever buy imported foods brought by ship from distant ports?

_____

Most commentators see in this passage an indication of frugality. Are you a thrifty home manager? Explain.

_____

_____

_____

Look up the following verses and share which stand out to you and why.

Proverbs 21:20

_____

_____

_____

_____

_____

Luke 15:13

_____

_____

_____

_____

Luke 16:1-2

_____

_____

_____

_____

_____

Do you like to go grocery shopping? How might you change your thinking to make it a more pleasant experience?

_____

_____

_____

Why is food so critical?

_____

_____

_____

Share what is important to you concerning food and meals.

_____

_____

_____

Does your family eat its meals together?

_____

Proverbs 13:25 in *The Living Bible* paraphrase warns us of the danger of "living to eat." Summarize your thoughts after reading each of these verses: **Job 23:12b ■ Psalm 119:103 ■ Proverbs 25:16 ■ Proverbs 25:27 ■ Ecclesiastes 6:7 ■ Jeremiah 15:16 ■ Matthew 4:4 ■ Luke 12:21-22 ■ John 4:34 ■ Romans 14:17 ■ 1 Corinthians 10:31.**

_____

_____

_____

_____

Do you think this verse means that a husband should never do any of the grocery shopping? Explain.

_____

_____

_____

_____

_____

_____

_____

7

HER PREPARATIONS

She also rises while it is yet night, And provides food for her household, And a portion for her maidservants.

Proverbs 31:15 (NKJV)

After you answer all the questions below, come back and give a banner heading to verse 15.

Do you think of yourself as a "morning person" or an "evening person"?

Do you think this pattern is hard-wired into your brain or is it something that can change?

If you think it can change, how would it be possible to reset your internal biological clock?

Do you have maids? If so, how many?

Read Proverbs 27:23-27. How would this section of Proverbs connect with Proverbs 31:15?

What "flocks and herds" has God given you to care for? What shape are they in?

_____

_____

_____

According to 1 Peter 5:2, what heart attitude did Peter admonish in the Shepherds of the Household of God?

_____

_____

_____

Share honestly about your own heart attitude concerning how you watch over those for whom you are responsible.

_____

_____

_____

_____

_____

How does Philippians 2:4 help us guess at this good woman's reason for rising so early?

_____

_____

_____

_____

Would anyone ever call this good woman *indolent*? Look up that word and the following verses. Which particular verse really stands out to you, and why?
Proverbs 6:9-11 ■ Proverbs 19:15 ■ Proverbs 20:13■ Proverbs 24:33-34

_____

_____

_____

_____

What are some good reasons for getting up before everyone else in your household awakens?

_____

_____

_____

Name some reasons why people have trouble getting up early in the morning?

_____

_____

_____

In what way does Proverbs 31:15 indicate that this good woman is like Jesus in Mark 1:35?

_____

_____

_____

Juanita Hall

8

HER STEWARDSHIP

She considers a field and buys it; From her profits she plants a vineyard.
Proverbs 31:16 (NKJV)

After you answer all the questions below, come back and give a banner heading to verse 16.

_____

_____

If you had some money to invest, what would you invest it in?

_____

Check out Proverbs 21:20, and ask the Lord if you are generally wise or foolish in how you spend your money, and that of your household. Do you think you have learned how to handle money well? If so, on what do you base your answer?

_____

_____

_____

Do you think about biblical stewardship? If so, do things like saving, balancing a checkbook or debit card ledger, budgeting, avoiding debt, investing, and providing for retirement fit into that, and if so, why? If biblical financial stewardship is not in your thinking, what could help you learn all those skills?

_____

_____

_____

_____

_____

What kind of mindset does it take to "consider, evaluate, assess, appraise, gauge, and calculate" a purchase?

_____

_____

_____

_____

_____

Are you an impulsive shopper?

What is the last big purchase you had to make? Were you happy with your purchase? Share about that.

_____

_____

_____

_____

_____

Look up the following verses and explain which verse stood out to you most, and why.
Proverbs 14:15 ■ Proverbs 19:2 ■ Proverbs 21:5

_____

_____

_____

_____

The Amplified Version of Proverbs 31:16 says that in making this purchase, *"she expands prudently and doesn't court neglect of her present duties by assuming other duties."* Why do we sometimes neglect present duties by assuming other ones?

_____

_____

_____

_____

_____

What might motivate us to assume new duties to the neglect of present ones, besides a time of truly inescapable need?

_____

_____

_____

_____

Share about a time when you have made that mistake. What were the consequences?

_____

_____

_____

_____

What *are* your present duties? Does Titus 2:4-5 help you find the biblical answer? Explain.

_____

_____

_____

_____

_____

_____

_____

Which of the following verses most stands out to you concerning not neglecting important things? Explain why.

Matthew 23:23 ■ 2 Thessalonians 3:11 ■ Hebrews 10:25

_____

_____

_____

_____

_____

Do you enjoy gardening? If not, does this mean that you are not a godly woman?

_____

_____

_____

What other cottage industries might be suitable for a woman at home with husband and children?

_____

_____

_____

_____

Read King Solomon's assessment of his gardening ventures. What makes the difference between a worthwhile and a meaningless enterprise, according to Ecclesiastes 2:4-6; 10-11?

_____

_____

_____

_____

_____

_____

Juanita Hall

9

HER STRENGTH

She girds herself with strength, And strengthens her arms.

Proverbs 31:17 (NKJV)

After you answer all the questions below, come back and give a banner heading to verse 17.

Is this verse saying that a godly woman needs to be a body builder?

The Revised Standard Version of Proverbs 31:17 translates the first words as "she girds her loins." That same Hebrew idiom is used in Exodus 12:11, 2 Kings 4:29, and 2 Kings 9:1. After looking up those verses, what insights do you gain about what it means to "gird up your loins"?

Read Genesis 24:1-20, focusing especially on verses 10, 19 and 20. How many thirsty camels do you suppose Abraham's faithful servant, Eliezer, had?

How many trips with her pitcher, from the well to the watering trough, do you think Rebekah had to make to fill up those camels?

What does this say about Rebekah's character?

Is all the manual labor that needs to be done in and around your home done by your husband or a paid worker, or do you do some of that work yourself? Describe what jobs you typically do, and how you "gird up your loins" in order to really get after the work.

When Verse 17 says, "She girds her loins *with strength*," what do you suppose is the source of that strength?

Meditate on the following verses (which all have the same word for "strength" that is found in Proverbs 31:17), and share about whichever verse stands out to you the most.

Psalm 28:7-8 ■ Psalm 29:11 ■ Psalm 46:1 ■ Psalm 59:16-17 ■ Psalm 62:7 ■ Psalm 68:35 ■ Psalm 84:5 ■ Psalm 84:5 ■ Psalm 105:4 (1 Chr. 16:11) ■ Psalm 118:14 (Ex. 15:2) ■ Psalm 138:3 ■

Jeremiah 17:7-8 (NLT)

But blessed are those who trust in the Lord and have made the Lord their hope and confidence. They are like trees planted along a riverbank, with roots that reach deep into the water. Such trees are not bothered by the heat or worried by long months of drought. Their leaves stay green, and they never stop producing fruit.

In Psalm 89:20-21, the psalmist quotes God as saying that He will "steady His servant David with His hand, with *His* powerful arm He will make him strong." (NLT) Do you ever have times when you feel that your own arms are limp and without strength? Look up the following verses to find clues concerning what actions can help you regain strength.

Psalm 89:20-21 ■ Hebrews 12:12 ■ 1 John 2:14 ■ Ephesians 3:16 ■ Colossians 1:11

Juanita Hall

10

HER SPIRIT

She perceives that her merchandise is good, And her lamp does not go out by night.

Proverbs 31:18 (NKJV)

After you answer all the questions below, come back and give a banner heading to verse 18.

_____

_____

_____

Check out how this verse reads in the Amplified version.

She tastes and sees that her gain from work [with and for God] is good; her lamp goes not out, but it burns on continually through the night [of trouble, privation, or sorrow, warning away fear, doubt, and distrust].

Proverbs 31:18 (AMP)

Do you sense that your gain from the work you do is good? Do you sense that there is eternal value in the work that you do? Is it profitable and worthwhile in advancing the Kingdom? Does it benefit your family and friends?

_____

_____

_____

How do the following verses encourage you?
Proverbs 3:13-15

_____

_____

_____

_____

Ephesians 6:7-8

Colossians 3:23-24

---

1 Corinthians 15:58

The word translated "perceive" in the NKJV literally means "taste." What do you need to "taste" first in order to "taste" that the yield from what you work at is good?

Psalm 34:8

---

1 Peter 2:2-3

_____

_____

_____

What other lamp mentioned in the Bible was never to go out, but was to burn on continually, even throughout the night? What fuel keeps the lamp burning?

_____

_____

What spiritually significant connection can you make as you look up the following verses?
Exodus 27:20-21 ■ Leviticus 24:1-4 ■ Matthew 25:1-13

_____

_____

_____

_____

What do the following verses indicate is done in the darkness, at night?
John 3:19

_____

_____

_____

1 Thessalonians 5:7

_____

_____

Romans 13:12-13

_____

_____

Verse 15 says that this godly woman gets up early in the morning, while it is still dark, and yet here in verse 18 we see that her lamp never goes out at night. Is this implying that she never sleeps at all?! What is your attitude when you are awakened at night?

_____

_____

But doesn't Psalm 127:2 warn us that it is vain for us to rise up early and stay up late at night? Explain.

_____

_____

What does Isaiah 5:11 say would be a bad reason for rising early in the morning or staying up late in the evening?

_____

11

HER HANDS

She stretches out her hands to the distaff, And her hand holds the spindle.
Proverbs 31:19 (NKJV)

After you answer all the questions below, come back and give a banner heading to verse 19.

_____

_____

Do you make your own thread and weave your own cloth? If not, then you'll never be a godly woman, right?

_____

What particular skills keep your hands busy?

_____

_____

Is there anything your hands are busy doing that they shouldn't be doing?

_____

_____

_____

Is there anything they should be busy doing that they're not currently doing?

_____

_____

_____

By doing a little detective work with our Bible program, and looking up the Strong's Concordance number for *hands*, we can discover more of what Solomon has to say about hands in the books of Proverbs and Ecclesiastes. What do the following verses say to you concerning the use of your hands?

Proverbs 3:27-28

Proverbs 6:10-11 (Proverbs 24:33-34)

Ecclesiastes 10:18

Proverbs 10:4

Proverbs 12:24

Proverbs 12:14

Ecclesiastes 9:10

Proverbs 19:24 (Proverbs 26:15)

Proverbs 21:25

_____

_____

_____

Proverbs 26:6

_____

_____

_____

Proverbs 30:32

_____

_____

_____

Proverbs 6:16-17

_____

_____

_____

_____

How does Exodus 35:25-26 describe these women who made a beautiful and quality contribution to the Tabernacle?

_____

_____

_____

How did the woman mentioned in Acts 9:36-42 make such an enormous impact on her community?

_____

_____

_____

Is it only the use of your hands that should concern you? How does Romans 6:12-13 instruct you concerning the use of every part of your body?

_____

_____

_____

Juanita Hall

12

HER HEART

She extends her hand to the poor, Yes, she reaches out her hands to the needy.
Proverbs 31:20 (NKJV)

After you answer all the questions below, come back and give a banner heading to verse 20.

_____

_____

The same hands mentioned in Proverbs 31:19 are still "reaching forth," only this time, toward what?

_____

Which of the following verses stands out to you and why?
Deuteronomy 15:7-8 ■ Proverbs 14:21 ■ Proverbs 19:17 ■ Proverbs 22:9 ■ Proverbs 28:27 ■ Matthew 25:34-40 ■ Luke 12:33 ■ Romans 12:13 ■ 2 Corinthians 9:9 ■ Galatians 2:10 ■ 1 Timothy 6:17-19 ■ Hebrews 13:16 ■ James 2:14-17 ■ 1 John 3:17

_____

_____

_____

_____

In Mark 14:7, Jesus quotes part of Deuteronomy 15:11 in saying that there will always be poor people in the land. Does that mean that it is useless to help out poor and needy people?

_____

_____

Should this good woman just indiscriminately help any and all poor people? Discuss how you decide whom to help.

_____

_____

_____

_____

_____

_____

If you were in charge of whether or not to monetarily help out a poor widow, would you even think twice about that? Read 1 Timothy 5:3-10 and write down how the Apostle Paul would help you with that.

_____

_____

_____

_____

_____

Some translations say that this generous woman "stretches out her hand" or that she "extends her hand" to the poor. In what ways do you "stretch out and extend" yourself in your giving?

_____

_____

_____

_____

Which of the following verses stand out to you, and why?
2 Samuel 24:21-25 ■ 2 Corinthians 8:1-5 ■ Luke 21:1-4

List practical ways we can reach outside our homes to help others.

Juanita Hall

13

HER COURAGE

She is not afraid of snow for her household, For all her household is clothed with scarlet.

Proverbs 31:21 (NKJV)

After you answer all the questions below, come back and give a banner heading to verse 21.

_____

_____

Are you afraid of snow? Does the thought of being snowed in at your house for two weeks make you feel anxious? What could you do to prepare your household for that kind of scenario?

_____

_____

_____

_____

Look up Proverbs 22:3 and 27:12 in some modern translations and paraphrases. How do they speak to you?

_____

_____

_____

_____

_____

_____

_____

What other kinds of scenarios frighten you? Be honest.

_____

_____

_____

According to Matthew 6:33-34, what *should* you be thinking about and doing instead of worrying about your own self-preservation?

_____

_____

If you are fearful about what *may* happen to you in the future, what does that reveal about you, according to 1 John 4:18?

_____

_____

Who is in charge of the weather? (Read the verses below.)
Job 37:6-7 ■ Job 38:22-23 ■ Psalm 147:16 ■ Psalm 148:7-8

According to Proverbs 31:21, who is in charge of seeing that the family is physically well-clothed? How do you take that assignment seriously?

_____

_____

_____

According to 1 Samuel 2:19, what was one way that Hannah showed her love to Samuel?

_____

_____

_____

_____

What is the significance of being "clothed in scarlet"? In Joshua 2:17-21, what color rope was critical in saving Rahab?

_____

_____

_____

After reading the following verses, discover what you and your family should be clothed in.

> **May your priests be *clothed with righteousness*; may your saints sing for joy... I will *clothe her priests with salvation*, and her saints will ever sing for joy.**
> **Psalm 132:9, 16 NIV**

> **I delight greatly in the LORD; my soul rejoices in my God. For he has *clothed me with garments of salvation and arrayed me in a robe of righteousness*, as a bridegroom adorns his head like a priest, and as a bride adorns herself with her jewels.**
> **Isaiah 61:10 NIV**

Read the following Scriptures, and explain how it is possible for us to be clothed with such garments.

Philippians 3:9 ■ 2 Corinthians 5:21 ■ Romans 1:17 ■ Romans 10:3-4

_____

_____

_____

Ponder deeply the words in Romans 15:13. What is the end result of being spiritually prepared, and walking in obedience to God in being physically prepared? Explain.

14

HER ATTIRE

She makes tapestry for herself; Her clothing is fine linen and purple.
Proverbs 31:22 (NKJV)

After you answer all the questions below, come back and give a banner heading to verse 22.

_____

_____

Are you a good seamstress or upholsterer? If not, does that disqualify you from being a woman of virtue?

_____

_____

Look around your house. What would it look like without your "feminine touch"?

_____

_____

Are you proud of the way it looks? Would you be comfortable with unexpected company?

_____

_____

What could you do to improve your home without incurring huge expenses?

_____

_____

_____

Do you think your husband is proud of the way you dress? What could you do to improve your wardrobe without incurring huge expenses?

_____

_____

_____

What is the significance of the color purple? (Research in a Bible Dictionary or Bible Encyclopedia.)

_____

_____

_____

What does Revelation 19:8 say is the "fine linen" we should be clothed in?

_____

_____

_____

_____

How do the following verses describe a true child of God?
1 Peter 2:9

_____

_____

_____

_____

_____

Revelation 1:6

_____

_____

_____

_____

_____

_____

Revelation 5:10

_____

_____

_____

_____

_____

_____

The Ruby Woman

15

HER INFLUENCE

Her husband is known in the gates, When he sits among the elders of the land.
Proverbs 31:23 (NKJV)

After you answer all the questions below, come back and give a banner heading to verse 23.

_____

_____

If your husband behaved in public today the way he did when you first met him, do you think anyone would respect him as a distinguished leader? Without throwing him under the bus, what kinds of things can you think of that you could do that might influence your husband in becoming a venerated leader in the community? Check out the verses listed below and share your insights.

Proverbs 12:4a ■ Proverbs 18:22 ■ 1 Timothy 3:11

_____

_____

_____

What are some bad ideas that you've seen some women try to do to push their husbands to the forefront?

_____

_____

_____

Look up the verses on the following pages to find ideas for how to pray for your husband; that God might be able to grant him honor as a respected leader. Without mentioning your husband's situation, share how the Scripture(s) helped you form a coherent prayer for him. Choose at least 5 of the verses.

1 Samuel 2:30

_____

_____

John 12:26

_____

_____

Proverbs 4:7-9

_____

_____

Proverbs 8:35

_____

_____

1 Kings 3:9-13

_____

_____

Proverbs 13:18

_____

_____

Proverbs 22:4

_____

_____

Matthew 20:25-28

_____

_____

Matthew 23:11-12

_____

_____

Proverbs 21:21

_____

_____

Matthew 5:19

_____

_____

1 Timothy 3:1-9

_____

_____

Titus 1:6-9

_____

_____

The main influences in your husband's life have contributed to his character development. Without naming personal names, who are those influences? Have they inspired him with all the good characteristics you are praying for, using the verses mentioned above?

_____

_____

_____

What does Titus 2:3-5 have to do with the main influence in your husband's life?

_____

_____

_____

Juanita Hall

16

HER EMPLOYMENT

She makes linen garments and sells them, And supplies sashes for the merchants.
Proverbs 31:24 (NKJV)

After you answer all the questions below, come back and give a banner heading to verse 24.

What involvement does this godly woman appear to have beyond the sphere of domestic life?

What does this suggest to you personally?

Name and describe the first Christian convert in Europe (see Acts 16:14-15)?

_____

_____

_____

_____

_____

Has one or more of your family ever gone without something because you over-spent household funds, or spent it in the wrong place? If so, what was the cost of such mismanagement or self-indulgence?

_____

_____

What do you feel is the best way for you to contribute to the finances of your family?

_____

_____

_____

_____

_____

17

HER DIGNITY

Strength and honor are her clothing; She shall rejoice in time to come.

Proverbs 31:25 (NKJV)

After you answer all the questions below, come back and give a banner heading to verse 25.

_____

_____

This is the same word for *strength* already covered in Proverbs 31:17. According to 1 Chronicles 16:27, where are strength and dignity (or honor) found?

_____

Using a good dictionary, define *dignity*.

_____

_____

_____

_____

_____

_____

What would be the opposite of dignity?

_____

_____

_____

How do the following verses, as read in the Amplified Version, relate to Proverbs 31:25?

And show your own self in all respects to be a pattern and a model of good deeds and works, teaching what is unadulterated, *showing gravity - that is, having the strictest regard for truth and purity of motive, with dignity and seriousness.* **And let your instruction be sound and fit and wise and wholesome, vigorous and irrefutable and above censure, so that the opponent may be put to shame, finding nothing discrediting or evil to say about us.**
Titus 2:7-8 **AMP**

The women likewise must be worthy of respect *and* **serious, not gossipers, but temperate** *and* **self-controlled, [thoroughly] trustworthy in all things.**
1 Timothy 3:11 **AMP**

How does the Proverbs 31:25 woman compare with the Proverbs 9:13 woman?

Webster says that one definition of *clothed* is, "provided and equipped and covered over, as if with a garment." What do you think those who know you best would say you are "clothed" with?

___ Innocence and naivety

___ Fear, suspicion, and insecurity

___ Foolishness and frivolity

___ Guilt and shame

___ Anger and bitterness

___ Sorrow, despair, and mourning

___ Pride and self-righteousness

___ Strength and dignity

Look up the following verses in the NIV translation. What have people been clothed with? Which verses stand out to you and why?

Proverbs 7:10 ■ 2 Samuel 1:24 ■ Job 7:5 ■ 1 Chronicles 21:16 ■ Psalm 30:11 ■ 2 Chronicles 6:41 ■ Psalm 132:9, 16 ■ Isaiah 61:10 ■ Ecclesiastes 9:8 ■ Luke 24:49 ■ Galatians 3:27 ■ 2 Corinthians 5:2

What goes through your mind when you are choosing what to wear each day? Is it a desire to gain attention and attraction, to look "hot" or trendy? What kind of person does that attract?

_____

_____

_____

_____

Do you think fashion trends were important to the Proverbs 31 Woman? Be honest; what do you spend more time on? Dress, hair and makeup, or the prayerful study of God's Word?

_____

_____

What advice on proper adornment does 1 Timothy 2:9-10 and 1 Peter 3:1-6 give?

_____

_____

_____

The Proverbs 31 Woman is clothed in strength. What is the opposite of strength? Comment on 2 Timothy 3:6-7.

_____

_____

_____

_____

_____

_____

Check off the circumstances of life of which you are tempted to be fearful.

___ Unexpected bills

___ Reduction or loss of income

___ Difficult job or home situation

___ Crippling injury, prolonged illness

___ Imminent surgery

___ Lack or loss of a relationship

___ Searching for a new church, job, home, etc.

___ Persecution, threats

___ Children leaving home; children's salvation

___ Hidden or past sin(s) being exposed

___ Old age care and impending death

Are you afraid of the future? Why or why not?

_____

_____

_____

_____

_____

What insight do you gain about the future from the following verses?
Psalm 37:12-13

_____

_____

_____

Psalm 37:37

_____

_____

_____

Proverbs 23:15-19

_____

_____

_____

Proverbs 24:14

_____

_____

_____

Jeremiah 29:11

_____

_____

_____

1 Timothy 6:17-19

_____

_____

_____

Matthew 25:19-23

_____

_____

_____

Matthew 26:64

_____

_____

_____

Romans 8:38-39

_____

_____

_____

Ephesians 1:16-18

_____

_____

2 Timothy 4:7-8

_____

_____

_____

Do you feel ready for the future? It seems that financial and other turmoil lie ahead because our culture has worshipped prosperity more than the God who blesses us with it. While nobody but God knows the exact future for each of us, what general things can you do to prepare?

_____

_____

_____

_____

How do the following verses speak to your heart?
Acts 21:13

_____

_____

Luke 12:35, 38, 40

_____

_____

Matthew 25:10

_____

_____

Revelation 19:7

_____

_____

Proverbs 21:31

_____

_____

_____

18

HER WISDOM

She opens her mouth with wisdom, And on her tongue is the law of kindness. (NAS, *She opens her mouth in wisdom, And the teaching of kindness is on her tongue.*)

Proverbs 31:26 (NKJV)

After you answer all the questions below, come back and give a banner heading to verse 26.

_____

_____

Most people live their adult lives barely existing, wandering around in the "desert" for 40 years, suffering the fallout of their parents' sins; and then they die. (Num. 14:33) They never live vibrant, eternally significant, victorious-over-the-giants-of-sin lives. That is not true of the Proverbs 31 woman. What eulogy would you like said about you at your funeral?

_____

_____

_____

Warren Wiersbe wrote, *"Remember that earlier in the book of Proverbs, Solomon used a beautiful woman to personify wisdom; this godly wife does the same."* (Proverbs 8) What is wisdom and where does it come from? Use Proverbs 2:6 and James 1:5 to write a definition for it.

Wisdom – _____

_____

_____

_____

_____

_____

So, I need to ask God—but how will He communicate with me? What answer can you get from 2 Timothy 3:14-17?

_____

_____

_____

_____

_____

_____

What is the connection between the following verses, and how do they apply to our study? **Proverbs 13:20 ■ 1 Corinthians 1:24, 30 ■ 1 Corinthians 12:8**

_____

_____

_____

_____

_____

When you open your mouth, does wisdom flow forth? Read Proverbs 18:4, Proverbs 15:2, and Luke 6:45 and share what you learn about the connection between the heart and the mouth.

_____

_____

_____

_____

What are the sources of the things that are stored in your heart (both good and bad)? Check out 1 Corinthians 3:19-20, Colossians 2:8, and 1Timothy 4:6-7.

_____

_____

_____

Okay, I need to read the Bible, and then I'll get smart, right? Is that all there is to it? Go to Psalm 111:2, 2 Timothy 2:15, Psalm 1:2, and James 1:25 and comment:

_____

_____

_____

I get it. If I study and meditate on God's Word, I'll learn what He's like, and what pleases Him. I'll also gain insights into myself, and human nature in general, right? What does Hebrews 5:13-14 tell you is also a vital ingredient in becoming a mature, wise woman who can understand the deeper things of God?

_____

_____

How do I know when to open my mouth and when to keep it shut? Who is speaking in Ezekiel 3:26-27, and why is it significant?

_____

_____

_____

What do you learn from Ecclesiastes 3:1, 7b; Proverbs 25:11, and Proverbs 15:23?

_____

_____

_____

_____

_____

What stands out to you most in the following verses, and why?
Psalm 37:30

_____

_____

Proverbs 10:31

_____

_____

Proverbs 4:5-9

_____

_____

Proverbs 1:8

_____

_____

_____

Deuteronomy 6:6-7

_____

_____

_____

Titus 2:3

_____

_____

_____

Would you agree with the following statements? "It's not what you say as much as HOW you say it," and "People don't care _what you know_ until they _know that you care_"?

Look up the following verses and comment on them.
Proverbs 19:13b

_____

_____

_____

Proverbs 25:24

_____

_____

_____

Proverbs 27:15-16

_____

_____

_____

Proverbs 21:9

_____

_____

_____

Proverbs 21:19

_____

_____

_____

Most would agree that every person's one great need is to be unconditionally loved and accepted by at least one special person who knows them intimately. Look up and comment on Proverbs 19:22 (especially in the Amplified) and Proverbs 20:6.

_____

_____

_____

_____

Define the word translated *kindness* in our study verse.

_____

_____

_____

_____

Would you agree that when you were dating your husband, you thought you knew him and loved him? But what happened when you got married? You were suddenly living under the same roof with this man whom you discovered did and said all sorts of things that you didn't know about before! You discovered all his flaws! Now that you are married to that "perfect man," your conversations and activities are less guarded. Neither of you work as hard at appearing at your best to try to make a good impression. (You only do that for other people, now.)

Reality has set in.

Then you had these adorable, perfect little children, right? Well, adorable, yes; perfect, no. You quickly discovered that they were born with a sin nature, "a curvature of the soul," as Haddon Robinson put it. We know this about our children, so we train them that their selfish behavior is unacceptable. Then we are surprised when they don't immediately, thoroughly, without question, and without complaint follow our every command! (Just like us with our heavenly Father, right?)

The question is, can we still have the "law of kindness" on our lips with our children, having discovered that they're not perfect, and never will be? Now that you know you're married to an imperfect man, with all sorts of hang-ups and insecurities, how are you going to treat him? It depends on how well you're able to remember the glaring faults, weaknesses, and insecurities in your own life.

Comment on these thoughts.

How well does God know you? Does He know all your faults and failures and weaknesses? Yet, how well does God love you? See Psalm 139:1-4, Act 1:24, Romans 5:8, and comment.

_____

_____

_____

Read through the following verses and pay close attention to the adjectives that describe the tongue. Which verses stand out to you, and why?

Proverbs 6:16-17 ■ Proverbs 12:19 ■ Proverbs 21:6 ■ Proverbs 26:28 ■ Proverbs 28:23 ■ Proverbs 6:24 ■ Proverbs 15:4 ■ Proverbs 17:20 ■ Proverbs 25:23 ■ Proverbs 17:4 ■ Proverbs 25:15 ■ Proverbs 10:20 ■ Proverbs 12:18 ■ Proverbs 18:21 ■ 1 Corinthians 13:1

_____

_____

_____

_____

_____

_____

_____

_____

19

HER WATCHFULNESS

She watches over the ways of her household, And does not eat the bread of idleness.

Proverbs 31:27 (NKJV)

After you answer all the questions below, come back and give a banner heading to verse 27.

_____

_____

How are the words "looketh well" in Proverbs 31:27 (KJV) translated in 2 Samuel 18:24-27 and 2 Kings 9:17-20? What insights do you gain?

_____

_____

_____

_____

_____

_____

_____

_____

_____

The New Living Translation says; **"She carefully watches everything in her household..."** In today's world, why is it key to keep a close eye on the conduct of your family and the condition of your home? What insight does Proverbs 15:3 give you on this?

_____

_____

_____

_____

We've already seen that the Proverbs 31 Woman provides physical and spiritual food for her household (Pr. 31:15), and that she is in charge of seeing that they are well-clothed (Pr. 31:21). Read the following verses and share which ones stand out to you concerning your own household, and why.

Proverbs 14:1 ■ Proverbs 7:11 ■ 1 Timothy 5:13-15 ■ Titus 2:3-5 ■ Proverbs 24:3

_____

_____

_____

_____

What is one area where the Lord is most asking you to work in regards to strengthening your family?

_____

_____

_____

_____

The word translated *idleness* comes from a word meaning *to delay, to hesitate, to be slow to go, to dawdle* (as in Judges 18:9). Are you characterized by being quick to obey the Holy Spirit's prompting when He places that certain good thought in your mind? Or are you characterized by procrastination? How does James 4:17 help you?

Read Proverbs 31:27 from the Amplified Version.

She looks well to how things go in her household, and the bread of idleness (gossip, *discontent*, and self-pity) she will not eat. *Proverbs* **31:27 AMP**

Many other verses in the Bible speak of being sluggish, lazy, slothful, indolent (avoiding work, indulging in ease), idle, slack; those who are slow to act through hesitation, disobedience, anxiety, negligence, or sloth. Meditate on the following verses and share which ones in particular stand out to you and why.

Proverbs 6:6-11 ■ Proverbs 10:4-5, 26 ■ Proverbs 12:24, 27 ■ Proverbs 13:4 ■ Proverbs 15:19 ■ Proverbs 18:9 ■ Proverbs 19:15, 24 ■ Proverbs 20:4, 13 ■ Proverbs 21:25 ■ Proverbs 22:13 ■ Proverbs 23:21 ■ Proverbs 24:30-34 ■ Proverbs 26:13-16 ■ Ecclesiastes 10:18 ■ Matthew 25:26-30 ■ Romans 12:11 ■ 2 Thessalonians 3:10-14 ■ Hebrews 6:11-12

The Bible tells of "the bread of affliction," "the bread of adversity," "the bread of tears," "the bread of sorrow," "the bread of mourners," "the bread of wickedness," and, in our verse, "the bread of idleness." One Webster's definition of "bread" is "support of life in general; that which sustains you." What "bread" is the support in your life? What sustains you throughout your day?

_____

_____

_____

_____

_____

How do Deuteronomy 8:3 and Matthew 4:4 relate to this discussion?

_____

_____

_____

_____

_____

In **John 6:33, 35, & 48,** and **1 Corinthians 5:8**, what kind of bread can we imagine the Proverbs 31 Woman eating that keeps her from eating the bread of idleness?

_____

_____

_____

_____

20

HER REPUTATION

Her children rise up and call her blessed; Her husband also, and he praises her: "Many daughters have done well, But you excel them all."

Proverbs 31:28-29 (NKJV)

After you answer all the questions below, come back and give a banner heading to verses 28-29.

_____

_____

List ways that your children bless and demonstrate respect for you.

_____

_____

_____

Since you reap what you sow, let's ask ourselves how we're treating our own parents. What grade would you give yourself? Brainstorm about ways to be a blessing to your aging parents.

_____

_____

_____

_____

_____

What is the Bible emphasizing in the following verses that would bless and demonstrate respect for an aging parent?

Matthew 15:3-6 ■ Mark 7:9-13 ■ 1 Timothy 5:8

_____

_____

_____

_____

_____

_____

Micah 7:6 ■ Matthew 10:21 ■ Mark 13:12

Instead of children rising up and blessing their parents, note what happens in the decadent society in which the Prophet Micah lived. Jesus said this would also be true in the end times when there would be very few morally and ethically upright people in the land. Is there any guarantee that all our children will rise up and bless us? Explain.

_____

_____

_____

_____

_____

_____

This woman's children, and her husband, realize that she is an outstanding mother and wife, and they tell her so. Do you think they always realized her value? What would make them realize her significance in their lives?

_____

_____

_____

_____

Verse 28 says that "her children call her blessed." Look up the word _blessed_ in the Strong's Hebrew Lexicon, or another Old Testament word study reference book, and define this word.

_____

_____

_____

_____

What does this woman do, how does she act that arouses and stimulates praise and admiration from those closest to her?

_____

_____

_____

_____

What motivates women to do noble things? Where does this woman get the strength of character that it takes to be steadfast in goodness, doing virtuously, nobly and well for people? The following verses help you find the answer. Briefly describe how.

Proverbs 31:30 ■ Proverbs 18:12 ■ Proverbs 21:21 ■ Proverbs 11:16 ■ Proverbs 3:35 ■ Philippians 3:10a ■ Acts 9:36

_____

_____

_____

_____

_____

_____

_____

_____

_____

_____

Remember that the book of Proverbs is a book of premises, not promises. It gives you guidelines and truth as a general rule, just in the same way you might advise someone that if they eat the right foods and exercise regularly they will live a long life. It is a premise, not a promise. Proverbs teaches that you can cultivate a heart for God in your child, so that when he reaches maturity he will have a ball and chain of God's grace on him that he will have to actively _fight_ to get away from (Pr. 22:6).

Of course God has given him free will and he must make his own choice to follow or not to follow Christ, but his strong conscience (filled with the truths of God's word, and knowing God's love that has been demonstrated through you) will make it awful tough to walk away from the Lord. How can you, as a mom, contribute to the likelihood that your children will honor and bless you in your old age? What key principle is found in the following verses that your children need to be taught?

Leviticus 19:3

_____

_____

_____

Exodus 20:12

_____

_____

_____

Deuteronomy 5:16

_____

_____

_____

Ephesians 6:1-3

_____

_____

_____

In the following list, underline the women whom you guess had children that rose up and blessed them? Explain why in the space below the list, on the following page.

- Hannah and her son Samuel (*1 Sa. 2:19*)
- Bathsheba and her son Solomon (*1 Ki. 2:19*)
- Maacah and her son Asa (*1 Ki. 15:13*)
- The Shunammite woman and her son (*2 Ki. 4:8-37*)
- Athaliah and her son Joash (*2 Ki. 11:1-3*)
- The Canaanite Woman and her daughter (*Mt. 15:21-28*)
- Eunice and her son Timothy (*2 Ti. 1:5*)
- Mary and her son Jesus (*Mt. 12:46-50, Jn. 19:25-27*)

_____

_____

_____

_____

_____

Do you think the Proverbs 31 Woman settled for mediocre in her life, or do you think she sought to excel and do her very best in the activities to which God had called her?

_____

_____

The husband declares that his amazing wife stands out among most other women. He believes her to be the best. Do you think your husband feels that way about you? Does he boast to others of the admirable things you do?

_____

_____

If you can't think of him praising you, what should your inner heart response be?

_____

_____

21

HER BEAUTY

Charm is deceitful and beauty is passing, But a woman who fears the LORD, she shall be praised.

Proverbs 31:30 (NKJV)

After you answer all the questions below, come back and give a banner heading to verses 30.

_____

_____

What do you think is meant by "charm is deceitful"?

_____

_____

_____

What do you think is meant by "beauty is vain"?

_____

_____

_____

Is there such a thing as a perfectly beautiful woman? Does she exist—perfect face, perfect figure, perfect personality?

_____

_____

_____

_____

What does 2 Corinthians 10:12 say about comparing ourselves to others?

_____

_____

_____

_____

According to 1 Timothy 2:9-10, what makes women who claim to be devoted to the Lord attractive?

_____

_____

_____

What is the beautiful woman in Proverbs 11:22 lacking?

_____

According to 1 Peter 3:3-5, how can women whose hope and trust is in God beautify themselves?

_____

_____

_____

What does God value and how does He judge a person (1 Sa 16:7)?

_____

_____

_____

According to the following verses, how is inner beauty cultivated?
Psalm 27:4

_____

_____

_____

2 Corinthians 3:18

_____

_____

_____

2 Peter 1:2-4

_____

_____

_____

Psalm 149:4 NKJV says, **"For the LORD takes pleasure in His people; He will beautify the humble with salvation."** How does salvation beautify you?

_____

_____

_____

_____

Are you sad because you no longer have the figure you had in your earlier years? Are you beginning to feel like your body is falling apart? What encouragement is found in 2 Corinthians 4:16?

_____

_____

_____

_____

According to Proverbs 31:30, what is this godly woman's motivating factor for all the good things she does and says?

_____

_____

_____

Does "the fear of the Lord" mean cowering in terror of Him? What does it mean?

_____

_____

_____

Why does the Lord want us to fear Him? What insight does each of the following verses give you on fearing God?

Jeremiah 32:38-40

_____

_____

_____

Proverbs 1:7

_____

_____

_____

Proverbs 14:27

_____

_____

_____

Ecclesiastes 12:13

_____

_____

_____

What do each of the following verses say are the guaranteed results of not seeking the fear of the Lord?

Proverbs 1:28-31

_____

_____

_____

Proverbs 28:14

_____

_____

Ecclesiastes 8:12-13

_____

_____

Psalm 119:120

_____

Hebrews 10:26-31

_____

Galatians 6:7-8

_____

How can I learn to fear the Lord, the easy way, according to Proverbs 2:1-5?

_____

What will the woman in Proverbs 31:30 be praised for?

_____

What advice would you give to a man who is looking for a beautiful bride?

_____

_____

_____

_____

22

HER REWARD

Give her of the fruit of her hands, And let her own works praise her in the gates.
Proverbs 31:31 (NKJV)

After you answer all the questions below, come back and give a banner heading to verses 31.

_____

_____

We read earlier (vs. 23) that "her husband is respected in the gates." Remind yourself what "in the gates" refers to. According to verse 31, what is happening "in the gates"?

_____

_____

Read verses 12-30 again and list some of the good deeds of the virtuous woman's life.

Verse 12 –

_____

Verse 13 –

_____

Verse 14 –

_____

Verse 15 –

_____

Verse 16 –

_____

Verse 17 –

_____

Verse 18 –

Verse 19 –

Verse 20 –

Verse 21 –

Verse 22 –

Verse 23 –

Verse 24 –

Verse 25 –

Verse 26 –

Verse 27 –

Verse 28-29 –

Verse 30 –

According to Proverbs 11:16a, who attains honor and respect? Describe this woman.

_____

_____

_____

_____

_____

Good deeds often bring honor and recognition. Which of the following verses stand out to you, and why?
John 5:28-29 ■ Titus 2:6-7, Titus 2:11-14 ■ Titus 3:8 ■ Titus 3:14 ■ Hebrews 10:24 ■ 1 Peter 2:12

_____

_____

_____

In light of 2 Corinthians 5:9-15, does doing good deeds, in and of itself, get us praise from the One who matters most in life? Explain.

_____

_____

_____

_____

_____

In light of the following Scriptures, describe the future of the immoral seductress, the evil woman, the promiscuous woman, and the prostitute; and those influenced by her:

Proverbs 2:16-19 ■ Proverbs 5:3-5, 8-11, 20-23 ■ Proverbs 6:24-29, 32-33 ■ Proverbs 7:4-5, 10, 22-23 ■ Proverbs 17:11 ■ Proverbs 21:12 ■ Proverbs 22:14 ■ Proverbs 23:27-28 ■ Proverbs 24:16 ■ Proverbs 24:20 ■ Proverbs 29:3 ■ Psalm 37:37

_____

_____

_____

_____

_____

_____

How has doing this study affected your life? What changes have you made?

_____

_____

_____

_____

_____

_____

ABOUT THE AUTHOR

Juanita Hall has been married to Calvary Rio Rancho's Senior Pastor, Robert Hall since 1970. Her passion is writing and teaching women's Bible studies, both to mid-high girls as a Sunday School teacher, and to women of all ages as the Women's Ministry Coordinator for nearly 30 years. Through insight into God's Word and confessions of her own inadequacies in raising her three children, Juanita helps women find hope and direction in loving their own husbands and passing on their faith to a generation facing more and more evil in an unloving world (Mat. 24:12). She is ardent about helping women live the fulfilling, fruitful, meaningful life that Jesus promised all disciples—a life with eternal significance and value (John 10:10).

Juanita Hall

NOTES

Juanita Hall

Juanita Hall

The Ruby Woman

48601199R00085

Made in the USA
San Bernardino, CA
30 April 2017